WHAT IF

Ruth Perry

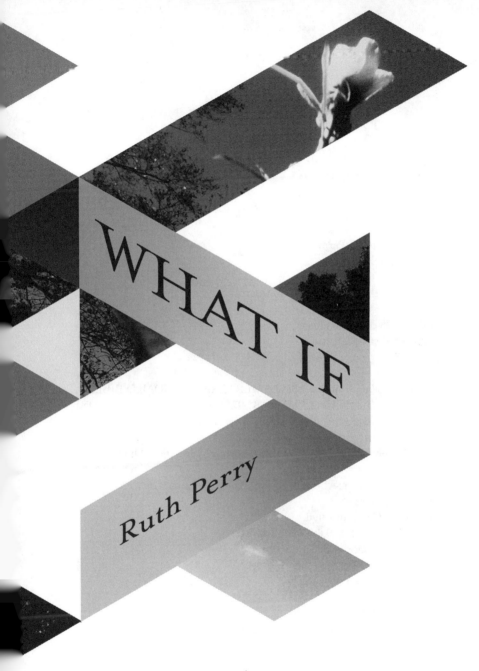

WHAT IF

Ruth Perry

AMBASSADOR INTERNATIONAL
GREENVILLE, SOUTH CAROLINA & BELFAST, NORTHERN IRELAND

www.ambassador-international.com

What If

Printed in the United States of America

ISBN: 978-1-62020-006-3
eISBN: 978-1-62020-007-0

Scripture taken from the NEW AMERICAN STANDARD BIBLE®,
Copyright © 1960,1962,1963,1968,1971,1972,1973,1975,1977,1995 by
The Lockman Foundation. Used by permission.

Photography, Cover Design and Page Layout by Matthew Mulder

AMBASSADOR INTERNATIONAL
Emerald House
427 Wade Hampton Blvd.
Greenville, SC 29609, USA
www.ambassador-international.com

AMBASSADOR BOOKS
The Mount
2 Woodstock Link
Belfast, BT6 8DD, Northern Ireland, UK
www.ambassador-international.com

The colophon is a trademark of Ambassador

ACKNOWLEDGEMENTS
To all my friends and family who allowed me to make a portion of their lives an open book so others may receive Christian encouragement in the journey of life.

CONTENTS

INTRODUCTION

THESE DEVOTIONALS WERE WRITTEN FOR the one who needs a little pep talk in discouraging times. I pray they will give motivation to change circumstances. "These things have I spoken to you so that My joy may be in you, and that your joy may be made full" (John 15:11 NASB).

Ten years ago my husband and I moved to a very rural area with no friends or family close by. I really needed someone to give me a pep talk! My husband had suffered a severe stroke and our life, as we knew it, came to a screeching halt. After managing some difficult changes, I realized we were not the only ones going through a life-changing event. Isaiah 43:2 says when we pass through the waters, God will be with us. If He leads us to it, He'll lead us through it! Praise God, He is still leading us today! Since that time I have found a wonderful church and have developed meaningful friendships. I pray this booklet will be of help to anyone needing encouragement.

My favorite verse in the Bible is found in John 16:33. "These things I have spoken to you, that in Me you may have peace. In the world you have tribulation, but take courage, I have overcome the world!" Did you hear that? He has already fought our battles for us! We just need to go through them to make our faith stronger in Christ and to give us a solid foundation IN HIM.

All the credit goes to God for giving me the inspiration for these pages. Without Him, these devotionals could not have been written. "I am the vine, you are the branches; he who abides in Me, and I in him, he bears much fruit; for apart from Me you can do nothing" (John 15:5; emphasis mine).

The Scriptures used in this devotional are from the New American Standard Bible unless otherwise noted.

A PIANO IN THE
BEDROOM

*But sanctify Christ as Lord in your hearts, always being
ready to make a defense to everyone who asks you to give an
account for the hope that is in you, yet with gentleness and
reverence.*

I Peter 3:15

AT OUR CHURCH WE HAVE altar invitations at the end of
services, where people who feel God's leading can come to the
altar and pray.

One evening during the altar call, I felt my son Jeff was trying to decide whether to go forward or stay where he was. I bent
down to talk to him about Jesus and ask if he wanted to go pray.
He was still hesitant, so I told him he didn't have to go to the altar
and that if he wanted, we could pray at his bedside when we went
home that evening.

Jeff's brother, Dennis, was six years old at the time, and
he heard me talking to Jeff. He was confused. Dennis whis-

pered to me, "But, Mom, who's going to play the piano in Jeff's bedroom?"

To Dennis, an altar call with a piano playing hymns in the background symbolized the way of salvation. This made me think of the times I had taught the younger children in Sunday school. Had I been using too many symbols in my lessons? Do they really understand what salvation means in their own simple language? From that day on, I made sure I spoke on their level whenever I was teaching them. "Let your light shine before men in such a way that they may see your good works, and glorify your Father who is in heaven" (Matthew 5:16).

What if we always make sure our lives this week are emitting the correct message of God? There are people, young and old alike, who are watching and listening to us. Be careful! Actions speak louder than words!

ACTUALLY LISTENING

He who restrains his words has knowledge, and he who has a
cool spirit is a man of understanding.

Proverbs 17:27

MY THREE-YEAR-OLD SON WAS HAPPILY playing outside next to the window I was washing from the inside. The window was open, so he started babbling to me. I continued washing the window, just answering his gibberish with "yes" and "is that right?" You know, the way we adults do to make children think we're listening to them.

When I looked up, I saw Dennis at the edge of the park on the other side of the highway, headed for the swings. My heart went to my throat. I dropped everything and ran out the door after him. As I caught up to him, I scolded him for going across the street.

I thought about the morning's incident. I realized he had asked if he could go play on the swings in the park and, unknowingly, I had given him permission. At that very moment I felt like a failure as a mother. I picked Dennis up, hugged him tight, and told him how much I loved him.

Do people see us as Christians who are too busy to listen? They talk to us, and we may say things like "uh–huh" and "I know" just to make them think we're listening when we're really thinking about what we're going to say next. People are hurting, and they need someone who will actually listen. We have the answer for their troubles! It's Christ! What an opportunity to witness.

What if when we have opportunity this week to listen to someone, we actually do? You know, the Lord only gave us one mouth but two ears. Maybe it's because He wants us to listen more than we speak.

BE READY IN ALL THINGS

Now may the God of peace Himself sanctify you entirely;
and may your spirit and soul and body be preserved complete,
without blame at the coming of our Lord Jesus Christ.
I Thessalonians 5:23

MY SISTER AND I SAT in a small airport and waited for our older sister to arrive from Colorado. Since it was a small airport, we assumed all the planes arrived from the eastern sky.

We were busy with our Sudoku puzzles when a voice asked, "Are you waiting for someone?"

Looking up, we saw our sister standing in front of us! "What are you doing here? We didn't even hear a plane!"

She laughed and said, "It came in from the west." We had been looking towards the east—when our attention wasn't focused on solving our puzzles.

The parable of the ten virgins came to my mind. "Then the kingdom of heaven will be comparable to ten virgins, who took their lamps, and went out to meet the bridegroom." The parable says that five were wise and put oil in their flasks along with their lamps, but the five who were foolish took no extra oil with them. The bridegroom was late, according to their timing, and they fell asleep. When it was announced the bridegroom was coming, the foolish wanted the wise to give them some oil, for their lamps were going out. But the wise had just enough for their own lamps, and the foolish had to go buy more. While they were gone, "the bridegroom came, and those who were ready went in with him to the wedding feast; and the door was shut." This parable is found in Matthew 25.

What if I live for God this week as if it were my last week on earth? "Be on the alert then, for you do not know the day nor the hour" (Matthew 25:13).

BIRTHDAY PRESENTS

These things I have spoken to you, that My joy may be in you, and that your joy may be made full.

John 15:11

LAST JULY WE HAD A birthday celebration for two of my grandchildren. I really love my grandchildren and want them to have good memories of their childhood when they are all grown up. So I try to make their birthdays special. I had the table decorated with fun stuff, and their dad baked a special cake for them.

Our tradition is to make the birthday kids' favorite dinner. So we had a macaroni and cheese gourmet meal given in honor of the two children reaching the ripe old ages of ten and twelve. After dinner, the cake and ice cream disappeared as quickly as the macaroni and cheese.

Oh, the joy of seeing them open their presents! They didn't really care what was inside. It was just exciting for them to tear the paper off and find out what the surprise was.

We should be just as excited when we think of God's present to us. He gave us the only Son He had because He so loved us. Did you get that? He didn't just love us but He so loved us! What more could we ask?

"For God so loved the world that He gave his only begotten Son that whoever believes in Him should not perish but have eternal life" (John 3:16).

What if I woke up every morning this week having joy in my heart knowing that God has given me the most wonderful present in the world? It would certainly make a positive effect on the rest of my day.

BLOOM WHERE YOU'RE PLANTED

Be anxious for nothing, but in everything by prayer and supplication with thanksgiving let your requests be made known to God.

Philippians 4:6

ONE MORNING I WAS TAKING my daily walk along a country lane. I usually use my walking time to commune with God, and this morning I felt a little down about things going on in my life. Also, there was the question in my mind if I was ever going to make friends in my new location. God directed my eyes to flowers in the ditch. I saw the most beautiful, delicate blue flowers in the middle of a patch of weeds. It had been extremely hot for nearly a month, and it seemed strange these little flowers could survive.

Then I thought about all the times in my life that my circumstances had changed. My husband's job would relocate to another town, or we saw opportunities elsewhere. We had three small sons, and I had to work outside the home, so it meant finding a babysitter in the new location. Leaving my friends behind was also tough for me because I had a difficult time making new ones. Paul said he learned to be content in whatever circumstances he was in. Thinking of this passage, I prayed for God to give me the courage to reach out to others, and I soon made new friends in a local church I attended.

"I can do all things through Him who strengthens me" (Philippians 4:13).

What if I make the most of wherever God puts me this week and bloom like those flowers in the road ditch? This would show others they, too, could reach out and trust God.

CHOICES

For what will a man be profited, if he gains the whole world, and forfeits his soul? Or what will a man give in exchange for his soul?

Matthew 16:26

I LIKE TO PLAY A GAME on the TV game channel called Spider. I have to move the cards around, placing them in mismatched places until finally I can maneuver the correct sequence of cards in the correct columns. Sometimes I win, but more often I don't. It challenges my thinking to try and make the right card move in order to get the end results I want, which is winning the game.

That game compares to our lives. We sometimes have to make choices that aren't what we really want in order to get the result for which we are striving. In Philippians 1:21-24, Paul has a difficult choice to make. He says, "For to me, to live is Christ, and to die is gain. But if I am to live on in the flesh, this will mean fruitful labor for me; and I do not know which to choose. But I am hard-pressed from both directions, having a desire to depart and be with Christ, for that is very much better; yet to remain on in the flesh is more necessary for your sake."

We're like a ship in the ocean. We are the ship, and the ocean is the world. The problem is not with the ship in the ocean, the problem begins with the ocean getting into the ship. This is why our choices need to be made only after we have prayed "God's will" be done!

What if I really think about the choices I have to make this week and choose the ones that would please God?

CONVERSATIONS

He leads me beside quiet waters. He restores my soul.
Psalm 23:2b-3a

I SPILLED MY HEART OUT TO a friend one afternoon as we traveled together. I really felt like I needed to talk. I went on and on. As I was talking to her, I realized she wasn't even listening to me! Her thoughts were a hundred miles away. I thought I was having a conversation with her, but I was the one doing all the talking. She got so tired of me droning on about my problems without giving her a chance to interject that she just quit listening! At that moment I came to understand that a conversation is a dialogue between two people, not one person doing all the talking and one person doing all the listening.

In Psalm 139:17, David says, "How precious also are Thy thoughts to me, O God!" That should also be our prayer. God wants us to talk with Him, but He also wants us to be quiet and listen so He can give us direction in our lives. When we have our devotions, we need to turn the television or radio off and give all of our attention to God. Don't worry about the phone ringing; whoever it is will call back. Don't think about what needs to be done. It'll be taken care of in due time. Our prayers are conversations with God. And do you know what? That's a local call! We can talk as long as we want without being charged for overtime on His plan! JUST TAKE TIME TO LISTEN TO GOD.

What if we give God our undivided attention this week, if just for sixty seconds when we are through talking to Him? What message might He share with us if we give Him our full attention?

COOKIE JARS

But now abide faith, hope, love, these three; but the greatest of these is love.

I Corinthians 13:13

MY SISTER-IN-LAW KNEW I LIKED collecting decorative cookie jars. For my birthday she gave me a large moose head cookie jar with its ears as the handles to open the top. It was adorable and became the table's centerpiece.

My grandson used to visit us often on weekends. We loved the energy this little five-year-old boy exuded. It was a Saturday morning, and my husband and I were sitting at the table doing crossword puzzles. This was our regular routine on Saturdays. Brent was sitting at the table also doing his Saturday morning routine, coloring a picture for our refrigerator.

We were deep in thought when Brent spoke up. "Hey, Grandma, think you're ever gonna find any cookies for that cookie jar?" Dale and I looked at each other and burst out laughing! It had never occurred to me to actually put cookies in it.

Because I love Brent so much, by nightfall that cookie jar had cookies in it, and Brent never had to ask that question at Grandma's house again!

I never forgot Brent's innocent little question. It made me stop and realize that outside appearance is not what makes the cookie jar a cookie jar. It's what is on the inside that counts. Love never fails or disappoints.

Chapter 13 of I Corinthians is called the love chapter. Part of it says, "Love is patient, love is kind, and is not jealous...bears all things, believes all things, hopes all things, endures all things. Love never fails."

What if my life is so full of Christ's love this week that no one will have to ask if I am a Christian? I am not a Christian because I call myself a Christian. I am a Christian because the Holy Spirit has filled me with God's love.

DIRECTIONS

Thy word is a lamp to my feet and a light to my path.
Psalm 119:105

WE HAD JUST BEEN TO Texas to visit my sister. Mother had helped me on the trip with my three small sons, ages four, five, and three months. This was my first long trip without my husband driving, so I wasn't very knowledgeable about interstates and their signs.

Somewhere in Oklahoma, a sign directed me to turn east to get on the interstate. I knew it had to be wrong because Nebraska was north—it said so on the map—and there was no way I was going to get there by going east! So I ignored it and just kept driving north.

Suddenly, a road sign read "turnpike ahead." I knew that was definitely wrong, so I turned around and drove back to the sign that confused me in the first place. There was that sign, again telling me to turn east, but I ignored it the second time and of course, ended up near the turnpike. The third time, I knew I was going to have to trust the sign, knowing all too well it was incorrect.

With little experience driving on interstates, I had never seen a cloverleaf intersection. I was really surprised when I circled around and drove right onto the interstate I needed! The Bible says, "For whoever keeps the whole law yet stumbles in one point, he has become guilty of all" (James 2:10). If I had obeyed all the signs of the road but ignored that one sign that said to turn east, I would not have made it to my destination.

What if I follow all of God's directions this week without having to know why?

DO WHAT I DO

The things you have learned and received and heard and seen in me, practice these things; and the God of peace shall be with you.

Philippians 4:9

PAUL HAD JUST EXPLAINED WHAT our minds should dwell upon if we are Christians. Then, as the Scripture says, he went on to tell the Philippians that if they looked at the way he lived and followed his example, then God's peace would be with them. WOW! That's quite a statement!

You can read it for yourself in Philippians 4. Would we be so brave as to tell our brethren in Christ to follow our example so God's peace would be with them?

Our minds are constantly being exposed to thoughts that are not always admirable. They come through the media, the Internet, our co-workers, friends, people in check-out lines, even our family members. Most of these are daily contacts. No wonder Paul says we have to stand firm in the Lord!

You ask, "How in the world can I keep from having negative and impure thoughts with all that I hear and see?"

An evangelist once told me, "You can't keep birds from flying over your head, but you can keep them from building a nest in your hair!" In other words, thoughts that are less than admirable are going to enter our minds, but we are not to dwell on them. Using God's strength, we can dismiss them and "dwell on these things"—whatever is right, pure, lovely, and admirable. This doesn't come automatically; it also says we need to "practice these things" (Philippians 4:9). Then God's peace shall be with you.

What if I live this week as if people are looking at my life and following my example so God's peace would be with them?

DOING IT MY WAY

Cast your burden upon the Lord, and He will sustain you;
He will never allow the righteous to be shaken.

Psalms 55:22

"NO, I CAN DO IT!"

Dennis was determined to tie his own shoes! He didn't know how because he hadn't been taught yet, but he thought if his older brothers could do it, then he could too!

He would work with those laces until I would get tired of watching him. Finally, after his frustration turned to tears, he would come to me and ask if I would tie them so he could go outside and play. I would reach down and show him how to hold the laces so he could learn. Then with a kiss and a hug, he was out the door to play with his friends.

This scene made me think of all the times we tell Jesus, "I can do it! I don't want to bother you with my little problems." Then we struggle on our own in vain to make things work only to become frustrated and yes, maybe even cry a little. In Hebrews 4:16 we read, "Let us therefore draw near with confidence to the throne of grace, that we may receive mercy and may find grace to help in time of need."

Believe me, as easy as it sounds to just ask, our sinful nature is not wired to think like that. We like to be independent. We like to make people think we can handle it when all God wants is for us to ask for help.

What if I go to Jesus with all my problems this week and just ask for His help?

EXPECT THE IMPOSSIBLE

The effectual fervent prayer of a righteous man availeth much.

James 5:16 (KJV)

LIVING IN THE COUNTRY WAS exciting for eight-year-old Carson and his sister, Kinley, who was six. They were outside playing when their dad called for them. Carson came running up to the house.

"Where's Kinley?" Dad asked.

"We found a dead cow out by the back fence, and Kinley's still out there!" he said, out of breath.

"Well, go get her. It's supper time," Dad told him.

But Carson said excitedly, "I can't, Dad! She's prayin' for the cow!"

Oh, the faith of a child! Being six years old, Kinley didn't know the cow was dead. She just thought it was sick, and she had just learned in her Sunday school class to pray for the sick.

Do you remember when Peter was in jail and the church was gathered in a home praying for his release? Acts 12:5 says, "So Peter was kept in prison, but prayer for him was being made fervently by the church to God." When Peter escaped with the help of an angel, he knocked on the door of that house. Rhoda the servant recognized his voice as Peter called out, but she didn't open the door. She was so excited that she ran to the prayer room to announce Peter was at the door! And how did they respond? Verse 15 says, "You are out of your mind....it is his angel." When they finally opened the door, they saw Peter "and were amazed." Do we fervently pray to God without really expecting an answer?

What if we come to Jesus with the faith of a child this week, honestly expecting Him to do the impossible? He can, you know.

FOLLOW MY PATTERN

Brethren, join in following my example, and observe those who walk according to the pattern you have in us.

Philippians 3:17

IS THERE ANYONE YOU KNOW whose life you would like to follow? My choice would be our pianist in a church I attended from my childhood through the young adult years. When I thought of angels in heaven, my thoughts always turned to Pauline. Her husband was the choir director, so she was also the accompanist for the choir. She taught Sunday school as well, and an encouraging word could always be heard coming from Pauline. Of all the years I knew her, I never heard a remark from her that would be displeasing to God. That's quite a legacy to try and follow.

My family and I visited them occasionally. And she always acted like she was the one being blessed by our presence in her home. By the way, she also made the best apple pie I have ever eaten!

When I think of Pauline, and I often do, I remember her as a wonderful, God-fearing Christian who always had a smile on her face and a testimony in her heart for her Savior.

Paul says, "Walk in a manner worthy of the calling with which you have been called, with all humility and gentleness, with patience, showing forbearance to one another in love" (Ephesians 4:1-2). This verse is the reflection of Pauline's life. She is my human pattern.

What if I made this verse my motto this week and hereafter so others can use my life as a pattern for their Christian walk?

FOREST AND
THE TREES

*Great is the Lord and highly to be praised; ...And on Thy
wonderful works, I will meditate.*

Psalm 145:3a, 5b

As we neared Mount Rushmore on our family vaca-
tion, I told the boys to look for the forest. We lived in the mid
plains, so they had never seen a forest except in pictures. My
sons were eight, seven, and three years old. As our auto slowly
climbed the mountain road with the hair pin turns, the two
oldest—knowing what a forest was—were oohing and aahing
over the huge trees. My three-year-old began crying. I asked
him what he was crying about. He sobbed, "I can't see the forest 'cause all these trees are in the way!"

Sometimes we don't see God's blessings right in front of us
because we are too focused on our problems. We think that God
has forgotten us. It reminds me of Habakkuk when he said in
chapter 1:2a, "How long O Lord, will I call for help, and Thou

wilt not hear?" God was listening. It just wasn't His time to answer yet.

In chapter two verse four, when God told him that "the righteous live by their faith," that seemed to be enough for Habakkuk. We read in 3:17-18 that though all things fail to reproduce, "yet I will rejoice in the Lord." Habakkuk got the trees out of the way and saw God's beautiful forest.

Take just a moment and look at God's beauty: the skies, the clouds, the trees and the flowers, the birds and the animals. Remember to thank God for everything and trust Him in everything. Our prayers will be answered in God's time.

What if we start looking for God's blessings this week and focus our thoughts on Him?

GENTLE TOUCHES

Instruct them to do good, to be rich in good works, to be generous and ready to share, storing up for themselves the treasure of a good foundation for the future, so that they may take hold of that which is life indeed.

I Timothy 6:18-19

HAVE YOU EVER FELT THE Holy Spirit's gentle touches? Sit with that person sitting alone in church. Visit that one who's homebound! Call on your neighbor. Phone that friend who's discouraged. The list goes on.

Maybe your answer is "I just don't have the time right now. If there's enough time after I run my errands, take care of all my appointments, pick my kids up from school, and get dinner started, then I'll see what time I have left to devote to it."

What is the Holy Spirit calling you to do today?

Martha was an example in the Bible of wanting to get her daily chores done first. Then she would have time for Jesus. In Luke 10:40-42, we read of the account. "But Martha was distracted with all her preparations; and she came up to Him and said, 'Lord, do You not care that my sister has left me to do all the serving alone? Then tell her to help me.' But the Lord answered and said to her, 'Martha, Martha, you are worried and bothered about so many things; but only a few things are necessary, really only one, for Mary has chosen the good part, which shall not be taken away from her.'" Just like Martha, we think we need to do our daily chores, but we shouldn't put God in second place to do them.

What if I obeyed the Holy Spirit's gentle touch this week instead of putting it off? Doing work for Jesus really is laying up treasures in heaven.

GIVE A HELPING HAND

Let us consider how to stimulate one another to love and good deeds, not forsaking our own assembling together, as is the habit of some, but encouraging one another, and all the more, as you see the day drawing near.

Hebrews 10:24-25

MY BROTHER AND SISTER-IN-LAW WERE visiting with their granddaughter, Callie. For a six–year-old, she was a very caring little child. My husband had to walk with a cane because of a stroke five years earlier. As he began walking back into the house from the porch, Callie was right there to assist him. Dale had to step up to go into the kitchen, and she put her hand on his leg. With both Callie and Dale in the small door frame, she said, "Okay, honey, just step up now."

Dale got so tickled he had to steady himself with his cane before he could take the step up. She just kept encouraging, "Okay, honey, you can do it. Just step up now." He finally composed himself and managed through the doorway with her small body next to his as Callie sought to help him accomplish the difficult task before him.   When he was inside, she beamed because she thought it was her encouragement and her little hand on his leg helping that made him able to get up the step! "Therefore encourage one another and build up one another" (I Thessalonians 5:11). A friend once told me that nothing improved her hearing like a word of praise.

What if we encourage our brother or sister in Christ this week whenever we have an opportunity to do so?

GONE FISHING

Follow Me, and I will make you fishers of men.
Matthew 4:19

DADDY LIKED TO FISH. HE was a hard worker, and we didn't get to go often, but when we did, it was an all afternoon event. Mother would fix a picnic lunch, and off we'd go to one of Daddy's favorite fishing spots. After he found a good one (of course, it was never in the shade), Daddy would first get the poles ready for my brother and me.

None of that fancy rod and reel stuff they have today. We used good ol' bamboo poles with bobbers. Out in the water they'd go, and then we would sit and sit and sit some more.

"Watch the bobber. When it goes under, yank on the pole." Those were the only instructions our Daddy gave us. We would usually catch enough fish for supper. But when we didn't, Daddy would always say, "We'll get 'em next time." We never grew weary of going fishing with Daddy.

We also need to have that kind of perseverance when we are praying for our family and friends to find Jesus as their personal Savior. Then we can say with Paul, "I have fought the good fight, I have finished the course, I have kept the faith" (II Timothy 4:7).

What if we remain patient and prayerful this week with the people we are burdened for who need to make a decision to follow Jesus? Think of it as sitting on the river bank waiting for the bobber to go under. We need to make a sincere effort to keep people interested in the Word of God until they make a decision to follow Jesus. You catch 'em, and Jesus will "clean" 'em!

GO TO THE SOURCE

All Scripture is inspired by God and profitable for teaching, for reproof, for correction, for training in righteousness; that the man of God may be adequate, equipped for every good work.
II Timothy 3:16-17

A FEW MONTHS AGO I SAT at my desk with the Bible open, a commentary beside me, and my Bible concordance ready as well as several other helpful study books. I was dissecting and examining every phrase. I started thinking about this scenario. Instead of reading God's Word and letting it give me direction, study books and self-help books were filling my thoughts!

Don't misunderstand me. It's a good thing to "study to show thyself approved onto God." But sometimes we get so involved in all the study books and commentaries that we forget to peruse the Bible itself. The devotional Scripture at the top of this page tells me that Scripture alone will make me adequate and equipped for every good work that I do for God.

With that thought in mind, I tried a little experiment. I started reading one of the Gospels just as I would a regular non-fiction book from start to finish. I wanted to see if I could understand the message just from the Bible's point of view. It was so good I am now reading each book as if it were the only thing I had available to learn how to live according to God's will for me.

What if we pray for the Holy Spirit to be our Interpreter and then read an entire Gospel this week and let God speak to us? If you don't know where to start, may I suggest the Gospel of John? I think you will be amazed at how much you will learn from the Holy Spirit's guidance.

GREATER IS HE

You are from God, little children, and have overcome them
(false prophets); because greater is He who is in you than he
who is in the world.

I John 4:4

I GOT ON THE SCALES, LOOKED down, and gasped. "Oh, no,
I've gained thirty pounds!"

I looked back on the last few months of my life. I was going
through a bit of a difficult time spiritually, and I realized I had
been feeling sorry for myself. It was winter. There's not a lot of
physical work to do here in the winter months. No one visits
in the winter, and I was a little lonely. So what had I done to
make things better? I found a good friend in peanut M&M's.
When I realized what I was doing to my body, I made some
drastic changes. The first thing, of course, was to stop buying
the candy, and the second thing was to sign up for a weight-loss
program. It took two months to put the weight on and two
years to get it off!

Becoming absent minded is the same way we get into trouble spiritually. We neglect to put on God's armor as He says

in Ephesians 6, and little by little, we let sin slip back into our lives.

Before we know it, we are lacking spiritual nutrition. We begin staying home from church services. We shy away from our Christian friends. We become withdrawn and melancholy.

Snap out of it! Reach out to God! Matthew 26:41 says, "Keep watching and praying that you may not enter into temptation; the spirit is willing, but the flesh is weak."

What if I devote myself to reading the Bible this week instead of substituting something that can hurt me?

HARD TO PLEASE

And let us not lose heart in doing good, for in due time we shall reap if we do not grow weary.

Galatians 6:9

HAVE YOU EVER HAD TO cook for a picky eater? Last winter our cousins came for a visit. That evening I fixed crab cakes because I knew Opal liked them. After dinner Lew informed me he wasn't much of a crab cake person. I gave my apologies and lightheartedly told him I'd try to do better tomorrow.

The next morning I fixed blueberry pancakes. After breakfast, Lew told me he didn't like blueberries in his pancakes. He then thanked me for keeping them in one cluster so he could pick them out easier. Ouch!

I told Opal I was planning to fix grilled cheese sandwiches to go with Lew's chili. She quickly replied, "Lew doesn't like cheese sandwiches." I give up!

That evening I asked Opal, "What would Lew like for breakfast tomorrow morning?"

She answered, "He loves cinnamon rolls." So I prepared rolls for the next morning. With the yeast dough mixed, I set it aside to rise. It didn't. The yeast was no good!

Donning my coat, I hollered in to Opal, "I'm headed for the store to get some more yeast," and was out the door before she could object.

This time I proofed the yeast. It was good, so I prepared the rolls and set them in the refrigerator to rise overnight. The next morning we had hot, sticky cinnamon rolls.

Lew exclaimed, "I'm sure glad you didn't give up on the rolls. They are wonderful!"

Mission accomplished!

What if we keep trying to do the right thing this week even when it seems like everything is set against us? God will give us credit even if no one else will!

HARVEST TIME

I sent you to reap that for which you have not labored; others have labored and you have entered into their labor.

John 4:38

As I was canning green beans, this Scripture came to mind. "I planted, Apollos watered, but God was causing the growth. So then neither the one who plants nor the one who waters is anything, but God who caused the growth" (I Corinthians 3:6-7).

I caught myself smiling at the memory of my kids, grandkids, and friends out in the newly plowed garden spot, carefully planting our garden seeds. Later, when it came time to pick, clean, snap, and can the green beans, where was everyone? No one wanted to be involved in the hot, sweaty work of harvesting. Harvesting isn't easy, but it's important for our survival.

Why, then, shouldn't I consider it even more important to be harvesting for Jesus? In John 4:35-36, Jesus said, "Lift up your eyes and look on the fields, that they are white for harvest. Already he who reaps is receiving wages, and is gathering fruit for life eternal; that he who sows and he who reaps may rejoice together."

Where are the harvesters? We are all busy providing for our families. While that is important, we need to make certain that we also give time to help with the spiritual harvest. Did you know God requires ten percent of our time also? There are 168 hours in a week. That would be 16.8 hours a week to return to Jesus.

What if we all dedicated ten percent of our time to Jesus this week? This includes Bible study, prayer, witnessing, calling, attending church, and more. When you think about it, ten percent of our time isn't very much time to give Jesus, is it?

HELPING OTHERS

In everything I showed you that by working hard in this manner you must help the weak and remember the words of the Lord Jesus, that He Himself said, "It is more blessed to give than to receive."

Acts 20:35

HAVE YOU EVER SEEN AN alpaca up close and personal? My friend Shirley hadn't ever seen one, so we visited the alpaca farm in our area.

When we arrived, we entered a small shop full of beautiful hand-knitted and crocheted shawls made from alpaca yarn. The owner was busy knitting. We struck up a conversation, and her story bears repeating.

Because of health issues, she lost her job several years ago. She had to go through two hip replacements and told us she was also a cancer survivor. She was so little I couldn't help but wonder how the doctors ever got two artificial hips in her! She had a determined attitude to do something for others, and when she saw the alpacas in an ad, she fell in love with them. Wanting to contribute to others, she told her husband this would be a way for her to give back to society.

They bought two alpacas. Seven years later, they have thirty-two alpacas with eight babies on the way! She feels blessed that the Lord has been so good to them. She opens her home weekly for ladies to come and fellowship while making prayer shawls to give to others.

We too can contribute to society. We can read to people in nursing homes or run errands for invalids. Brainstorm. Write down all the ideas you can think of and then develop one into a ministry—to God from you.

What if we made a commitment this week to help just one person in need?

I DON'T NEED INSTRUCTIONS

As you therefore have received Christ Jesus the Lord, so walk in Him, having been firmly rooted and now being built up in Him and established in your faith, just as you were instructed.

Colossians 2:6-7a

"I'M TRAPPED!"

These words from my husband, Dale, greeted me as I walked through the door of our home. Thinking he was just being funny, I smiled and went in to look at the mail.

Looking at me through the hole in the door where the doorknob was supposed to be, he said, "Sure, go ahead. Read the mail. I've been locked in this bedroom for over an hour."

Laughing, I peered back at him. "You mean you're not kidding? Why are you in that predicament?"

"I was trying to put a doorknob on this door, and the lock pin got jammed, locking it shut," he explained.

I asked where the instructions were.

"I don't need instructions," he replied. "It's just a simple doorknob installation."

I found a screwdriver and pried the hinges off the door, and he was soon free!

Another time, my husband tried to put together a small book stand. After he attached the bottom shelf and tightened the screws, he realized he had put the shelf on upside down. Reversing the steps he had just finished, he was able then to attach it correctly. Reading the instructions first would have prevented this.

My husband is mechanically challenged, shall I say, so he really needs instructions. This reminds me of the Scripture found in II Timothy 2:15. "Be diligent to present yourself approved to God as a workman who does not need to be ashamed, handling accurately the word of truth."

What if we study God's instructions and use them this week to help us stand against Satan's temptations? It will make a difference!

JUST RELEASE IT

Walk in a manner worthy of the calling with which you have been called, with all humility and gentleness, with patience showing forbearance to one another in love, being diligent to preserve the unity of the Spirit in the bond of peace.

Ephesians 4:1b-3

HAVE YOU EVER BEEN HURT by someone? You know, they say something to you or about you, and you get your feelings hurt. That has happened to me. I started feeling resentful to think someone thought a certain way about me. So I dwelt on it and climbed up the miff tree. Eventually I got over it enough to tuck it away in the corner of my mind for a later time—just in case I would need it to bring it up in the future and say "I told you." Of course, it became a stumbling block in my spiritual life.

I started feeling sorry for myself and began building resentment against that person. Instead of taking my problem to God, I held onto it and nurtured it until it created a spiritual problem in my life.

This is the same feeling of resentment Jonah experienced toward the people he had just preached to in Ninevah. They repented because of his words to them, and God felt compassion and forgave them, but Jonah didn't think they should have been forgiven. In Jonah 4:3-4 he says, "Therefore now, O Lord, please take my life from me, for death is better to me than life." You see, he was up the miff tree. The Lord said, "Do you have good reason to be angry?"

What if I just release any resentful feelings to God this week and let Him take care of them? What a freedom my soul will feel. Just release it and move closer to God.

KEEP ALERT

*Be on the alert. Your adversary, the devil, prowls about like
a roaring lion, seeking someone to devour.*

I Peter 5:8b

WE WERE HAVING A FAMILY fun day on the beach one sum-
mer. My husband, Bill, had brought a huge inner tube so that
he and my brother could use it to float on the lake. My boys and
I started digging in the sand, and by the time I looked up to see
where the men were, they had floated out of sight. I turned my
attention back to the kids.

A few hours went by. The boys were getting tired of playing in the sand and water, and I was also ready to go, but there
was no sign of the guys anywhere. Finally, I could see two men
carrying an inner tube down the road toward us. When they
finally arrived tired and sunburned, the story unfolded.

It was so peaceful on the lake that the men had closed their
eyes for a short time. When they opened them again, they realized they had floated out of their comfort zone! Using their
arms as paddles, the men paddled frantically to land. After walking an hour around a portion of the lake, they found us patiently

waiting. Bill and my brother had been caught up in the moment and took their eyes off their destination.

In our Christian lives, sometimes we get comfortable and take our eyes off our goal, Jesus Christ. Paul knew the importance of keeping watch. "I press on toward the goal for the prize of the upward call of God in Christ Jesus" (Philippians 3:14).

What if I keep my eyes on Jesus this week and press on toward the goal by staying alert?

LEAD BY EXAMPLE

"It is good not to eat meat or to drink wine, or to do anything by which your brother stumbles."

Romans 14:21 (emphasis mine)

A FEW YEARS AGO, OUR MINIATURE dachshund died. My husband revealed to me one morning that he really wanted another lap dog to keep him company. I told him I'd go online and see what our local animal shelter had ready for adoption. Immediately, a picture of a little five-week-old mutt popped up on the screen, and Dale said, "That's the one I want."

So we went to the shelter, and an hour later we were on our way home with Dale's lap puppy. She had the same markings as our German shepherd. Now, Trace didn't get along with other dogs, but I was hoping she would tolerate a puppy, and sure enough, she adjusted quickly to the new resident, Maggie.

As weeks went by, I could see Maggie would follow Trace, imitating whatever Trace would do. If Trace went outside to do her duties, Maggie followed. If Trace barked at the passing cars, Maggie followed suit. If Trace ate, so did Maggie, and on it went. Trace knew the basic commands—"come", "sit," and "stay"—and whenever I used them on Trace, Maggie would see what Trace did and act accordingly. In no time, Maggie knew and obeyed the words also. As far as Maggie knew, Trace was her mom.

Just as Trace was unknowingly an example for Maggie, the same thing is usually true in human lives. Paul said in I Corinthians 6:12, "All things are lawful for me, but not all things are profitable."

What if I live my life this week believing I am an example for that new "babe in Christ"?

LISTEN AND LEARN

Let us therefore draw near with confidence to the throne of grace, so that we may receive mercy and may find grace to help in time of need.

Hebrews 4:16

My son decided he wanted learn how to can potatoes, so I placed the instruction booklet on the counter for him to use. I helped peel and cut the potatoes so they would fit into the jars. With the jars in the hot water and another pot ready for pouring the water over the potatoes, we were ready.

As he was working, I noticed he didn't get the salt in all the jars as instructed. He also tried to fill the jars too full, and I explained why that wouldn't work. When he placed the potatoes in the canner and sealed the lid to start the canning process, he told me he had forgotten to check the water to make sure the correct amount was in the canner. Dennis didn't know I had checked it earlier because I could see he was not using the instruction booklet. Not having worked with a pressure canner before, Dennis didn't realize the drastic results that could happen if not used properly. A man I knew was canning meat one day, and he didn't watch the pressure gauge. He even ignored it to go do something else. All of a sudden, there was an explosion. The pressure had gotten so high that the canner lid had exploded! Meat adorned his entire kitchen! I didn't want something similar to happen in my kitchen.

I was reminded of all the times we don't know the answers to our problems. What do we usually do? We do what we think is best or, worse yet, ignore the problems and as a result cause more problems.

Psalm 55:22 says to "Cast your burden upon the Lord and He will sustain you; He will never allow the righteous to be shaken."

What if when we have a problem this week, we take it to the Lord first? He's been watching us all along anyway, just waiting for us to call on Him.

LOVE THE UNLOVELY

I tell you the truth, whatever you did for one of the least of these brothers of mine, you did for me.

Matthew 25:40, NIV

SITTING AT A KANSAS CITY bus station on a lengthy layover, I noticed a woman. She pulled a metal cart with teddy bears atop. Since she came in and out of the station, I assumed she was a homeless person. She was always chastising these bears for something they had done wrong. Of course, we all kept our safe distance.

Finally, my bus arrived. I noticed the Bear Lady getting on too. It turned out to be a long five-hour ride. Besides constantly scolding her "children," whenever the bus stopped, she tried to get off the bus to get some air. Of course, the bus schedule didn't allow time for that, so at each stop an argument ensued with the driver.

Omaha was another lengthy layover. As soon as we exited the bus, she hit the city sidewalks. When she returned, she slept with her "children" in her arms until the next bus arrived.

When the bus arrived, I found a seat on the front row next to the door and hoped to get some much-needed sleep. The Bear Lady asked if she could sit next to me. I said yes and asked what she was going to do with her bears. Immediately, she got up and went to another seat and said she would be out of the way there.

Guilt swept over me. Why didn't I just offer her acceptance? I prayed silently for God to forgive me and help me to accept people as they are.

What if we open our arms to people this week who need our acceptance and offer them God's love? God expects it of us.

MAKING GOOD
USE OF TIME

There is an appointed time for everything. And there is time
for every event under heaven.

Ecclesiastes 3:1

A FRIEND OF MINE MADE ME promise that I would start a
walking regimen every morning. He exercises regularly and
knows what a help it is for the body. After my first week of
walking up a hill (what was I thinking?) and then back home, I
have already seen results! My jeans are fitting looser at the waist,
and I'm not as tired. I have already felt the results too, but as they
say, no pain, no gain, right?

I have tried to do exercises in my home, but I really don't
like it, and so I would quit after a few days. This time I am
determined to keep the promise because of the benefits I will
receive from it. It costs me no money, and it only takes twenty
minutes of my time. Of course, I've just seen a small result, but
if I make this walking routine a habit, in a few short months I
am going to see big results coming from my exercise program.

I'm excited about it. As a matter of fact, God has already blessed me. I have made this my quiet time with Jesus, and it has become the best twenty minutes of my day.

I don't want my words to be like the Scripture describes in Proverbs 25:14a, "like clouds and wind without rain is a man who boasts … falsely." I want to follow through on what I promised. This is what God expects of each of us.

What if I tackle my daily responsibilities this week with the same determination I have with my walking? My time is actually God's. I need to be a good steward of it.

MAKING THE MOST OF A BAD SITUATION

Do not be discouraged, for the Lord your God will be with you wherever you go.

Joshua 1:9b, NIV

MY GRANDDAUGHTER KINLEY AND I took a mini vacation with my friend Shirley and her granddaughter, Whitney. The two girls made an instant connection that became a friendship.

At the motel, Kinley and Whitney immediately focused on the pool, and only minutes later, they were splashing in it. Shortly after their fun started, it ended! The visiting pool expert told me that the pool water was unsanitary. The girls were disappointed but soon found other entertaining things to do. Nothing was going to ruin their vacation.

The next day we went to KidsZone. After we had paid admission and gone inside, we discovered the activities were for much younger children than our tween-age girls. Did they complain? Not at all! They went to each play area and engaged in the activities with the smaller children. Again, nothing was going to ruin their vacation.

In the afternoon, we drove to an activities park where swan paddle boats were available to rent. A rain cell was approaching the city, and the girls only had fifteen minutes to use the paddle boat. They paddled with all the energy they could muster and enjoyed the few minutes they had on the lake. Once more, nothing was going to ruin their vacation.

My favorite verse came to mind. "These things I have spoken to you, that in Me you may have peace. In the world you have tribulation, but take courage; I have overcome the world" (John 16:33).

What if we accept all things this week without grumbling and arguing? In Philippians 2:14, God says we will then appear as lights in the world. How wonderful is that?

MY NAMESAKE

Let no unwholesome word proceed from your mouth, but only
such a word as is good for edification according to the need of
the moment, that it may give grace to those who hear.

Ephesians 4:29

IN THE LIVING ROOM WERE four baby girls. Their ages ranged from four years to a three-month-old infant. These were my brother's grandchildren by his daughter. My brother's son came to visit later with his wife and their three-month-old baby girl.

When they arrived, my brother took that little girl in his arms and hugged and kissed her, saying, "This is my first true little granddaughter because she has my name."

My jaw dropped open. Did I just hear what I thought I heard? I couldn't believe he said that with his daughter still sitting there, her children playing at her feet. Just because their last name was not his last name didn't make them any less his "true little granddaughters"!

No one said anything at the time, but later I mentioned the incident to my brother. Of course, he hadn't realized what he had actually said and immediately apologized to his daughter for his misplaced words. Darrell has a heart of gold and didn't mean to say something that could have been very hurtful had his daughter taken it to heart.

How often have I caused someone pain by saying something without thinking first? I think we've all been guilty of "foot–in-mouth disease" at one time or another! I ask God to forgive me for those times, for I know we are always to speak with love and grace.

"If anyone thinks himself to be religious, and yet does not bridle his tongue but deceives his own heart, this man's religion is worthless" (James 1:26).

What if my thoughts are so directed by God this week that I will know when to keep silent?

NEEDS BEING MET

All Scripture is inspired by God and profitable for teaching.
II Timothy 3:16

IT WAS THE FIRST LESSON in a new book study in our Sunday school class. The one conducting the lesson made a startling remark. "Until this study lesson, I had been considering dropping out of church attendance for one year."

Someone asked, "Why would you do that?"

She replied, "Because my needs weren't being met!"

This conversation really left me unsettled. The first thought that came to my mind is the verse that states, "It is not those who are healthy who need a physician, but those who are sick; I did not come to call the righteous, but sinners" (Mark 2:17).

After our teacher made that remark, she continued to say that we as Christians need to do all we can in our church to help the ones who are sick of sin and need Christ as their Savior. She is so right.

A question to ask ourselves: are we serving in the area where Jesus wants us to be serving? As an example, instead of attending a Sunday school class, ask God if you should be teaching a class. The Bible says we, as His followers, are to be doers of the Word and not just listening to the Word.

Sometimes we use so many popular best-selling books for our studies, we forget that the Holy Bible is THE Book to be learning from and using as our example for our Christian living. I'm not saying it's wrong to use those other books. Just don't use them in place of your Bible for devotions and Bible study.

What if we only use God's Word as our inspiration this week? If He can't inspire us, who can?

NEVER FORSAKEN

Brethren, even if a man is caught in any trespass, you who are spiritual, restore such a one in a spirit of gentleness; each one looking to yourself, lest you too be tempted. Bear one another's burdens. (emphasis mine)

Galatians 6:1-2a

My first marriage of twenty-one years was in trouble. We tried Christian counseling but, due to the chain of events that followed, divorce became the only solution. Two of my sons were grown, and my youngest son was fourteen years of age. The divorce was very hard for him to understand. In hind sight, I could have done things quite differently. I would never recommend divorce to anyone! Satan is so deceitful!

I relocated and found myself in a much larger church environment. I taught Sunday school and attended church services faithfully, but after sixteen months, I became disenchanted with everything. The people weren't friendly, and I was lonely. I became bitter towards the church. Taking my eyes off Jesus, I developed "I" trouble and fell into a backslidden state.

For twenty years I followed the worldly crowd, each night returning to my apartment, still lonely. During those years of wandering in the desert, I remarried. Of course, finding a Christian husband was not my priority. As man and wife, Dale and I wandered in the desert together. In our fifteenth year of marriage, my husband had a severe stroke. We retired to the Ozarks. Talk about lonely! One December I decided I'd had enough of doing things my way. I promised myself I was going to find a church and start attending.

I found my Bible, and it opened to Jeremiah 31:3. "I have loved you with an everlasting love; therefore I have drawn you with loving kindness. Again I will build you and you shall be rebuilt."

I started talking to the Lord, praying for forgiveness, and He rebuilt me. To make a long story short, I found a wonderful church, and Christ once more reigns in my heart. My husband Dale attends with me, and God has also given him a clean heart. God says He will never desert us nor forsake us, but we can let Him down by our unfaithful actions.

What if, when we get in dire straits, we immediately take it to the Lord? Much unnecessary heartache will be avoided!

NEVER GIVE UP!

Yet those who wait for the Lord will gain new strength, they will mount up with wings like eagles, they will run and not get tired, they will walk and not become weary.

Isaiah 40:31

THERE IS A YOUNG MAN who lives on our farm. We think of him as our adopted son, although we met him when he was already grown. Travis has a great sense of humor and a strong sense of perseverance. Travis doesn't have a personal relationship with God, but he has taught me not to give up on something I believe in. I pray for his salvation daily, and I have no doubt God will answer this prayer in His time.

Due to some unfortunate circumstances, Travis served some time in prison. While there, he heard of a job opportunity, and when he was released, he began pursuing it. The money sounded fantastic. If hired, it would give him college funding for his children.

After listening to his stories for about a year, we began to think it was only a pipe dream. Travis kept telling us they were working on it. We'd just nod our heads in agreement and think pipe dream. Travis never gave up hope.   It took two years of perseverance and finally, after several weeks of paperwork and training, he is now employed by the company!

What if I pursue my Christian endeavors this week with perseverance and determination?

Then at the end of my life I can say with Paul, "I have fought the good fight, I have finished the course. I have kept the faith; in the future there is laid up for me the crown of righteousness, which the Lord, the righteous Judge, will award to me on that day" (II Timothy 4:7–8a).

NURTURING THE YOUNG

A new commandment I give to you, that you love one another,
even as I have loved you, that you also love one another. By
this all men will know that you are My disciples, if you have
love for one another.

John 13:34-35

HAVE YOU EVER WATCHED MOTHERS as they care for their
babies? When the babies start crying, the mothers will change
their diapers, feed them, or comfort them. The mothers watch
the infants in the play pen to make sure they stay safe. As their
children grow into toddler stage, the mothers continue to make
sure they eat the correct food and have clean clothes. When
they are playing, the mothers keep watch over them. They are
ever under the watchful eye of their caring mothers. Because of
each mother's love for her children, she would do anything to
protect them.

We need to be aware of the new Christians in our church
and keep watch over them as a mother with her young. These

newborn in Christ get discouraged very easily and need nurturing from mature Christians.

Paul wrote in I Corinthians 3:2, "I gave you milk to drink, not solid food; for you were not yet able to receive it. Indeed, even now you are not yet able." He was speaking of the newborn in Christ. There are young Christians in church today who desperately need further nourishment. Not just from the pastor but from us, the laypeople.

What if we nurture the babes in Christ in our local church this week as if they were our own flesh and blood? If there was ever a need to help the young Christians in the church, it is today!

OVERDRAFT PROTECTION

But seek first His kingdom and His righteousness; and all
these things shall be added to you. (emphasis mine)
Matthew 6:33

OVERDRAFTED AGAIN! I COUNTED NINE times that my
friend used his debit card when there was no money in his account. Even though he had overdraft protection, each time he
used his card with insufficient funds, the bank assessed charges
to him. Since I was supervising his account, I told him I was
going to cancel the protection service if he continued to abuse
it.

Our spiritual banks work in the same way. Once in awhile
we may get so busy that we put off reading our Bible until later
in the day. And that usually means it doesn't get done. It's the
same way with our prayer time. We tell ourselves we'll pray
later when we have more time. God still watches over us and
loves us. He never forsakes us. But we don't have that com-
munion with God that we have when we read His Word every

morning. Read Matthew 6:25-33. It tells us what things will be added to us if we "seek first His kingdom."

Also, we might not have the "pray without ceasing" attitude God gives us to get through the day if we delay our devotions until later. Jesus still gives us His protection service and covers us with His grace, but our prayer time could become overdrawn or put us in a weakened spiritual condition, unable to be used of Him throughout the day.

What if I am determined that no matter how busy my days are going to be this week, I will read my Bible and pray to my Savior first thing each morning? Believe me when I tell you the rest of the day will go much easier!

PLEASING GOD

Whoever speaks, let him speak, as it were, the utterances of God; whoever serves, let him do so as by the strength which God supplies; so that in all things God may be glorified through Jesus Christ.

I Peter 4:11a

MY SON JEFF WAS FIVE years old when he decided to surprise me and clean the bathtub all by himself. When I checked to see if he was finished with his bath, I got quite a shock. There was Jeff, standing in the tub with half a can of Ajax cleanser dumped all around him!

After washing Jeff again, I sent him to the living room to talk with his dad. Then I started the process of cleaning the tub. I realized Jeff was just trying to please me, not knowing the extra work he had caused.

This reminded me of how we get so excited when we come up with a project we think will please God. Without talking to anyone or praying to God to make sure it's really His will, we plunge in head first. We want to please God so much that sometimes we get ahead of His timing. When this happens, things don't work out so well.

It always makes God happy when we want to serve Him, but we need to remember to wait on the Lord for His help, because our strength comes from Him! Psalm 37:7a says, "Rest in the Lord and wait patiently for Him." In Psalm 37:3-7, there are four key words I use to find God's will. The words are trust, delight, commit, and rest.

What if I trust the Lord this week to see if I am in God's will before I commit to my plans? If He wants me to proceed, it will be accomplished.

PREPARE THE SOIL

And the seed in the good soil, these are the ones who have heard the word in an honest and good heart, and hold it fast, and bear fruit with perseverance.

Luke 8:15

"DON'T ASSUME YOU ARE GOOD soil. A relationship with God simply cannot grow when money, activities, addictions, or commitments are piled on top of it." These words come from chapter four of the book called Crazy Love, written by Francis Chan.

I read this book with my jaw dropping in every chapter! One chapter is about "Lukewarm Christians." Just try to read that chapter and walk away feeling satisfied with yourself! Believe me; I had a one-on-one with Jesus after reading it!

I attend church services faithfully. I pray and tithe and volunteer at church when asked, but living in a rural area on a small retirement, what else could I do? In the back of my mind, there was always the thought that I could volunteer for a certain ministry in the area. Its specific cause is to help victims who have lost all or most of their belongings in a fire. But then I would start thinking, "What if something else came up I'd rather be doing—like going somewhere with my friends?"

Then I read Crazy Love. I knew some changes were going to have to be made in how I perceived living for Jesus. After the one-on-one with Jesus as previously mentioned, I reached for the telephone and called Angel's Home. The woman gladly and tearfully accepted my volunteer help. I am still God's work-in-progress, but like Mr. Chan wrote, the "good soil" is the Christian helping God to "grow the seed" that is bringing people to Christ. I want to be that good soil. That is what God has commissioned us to do!

What if we think of each person with whom we come into contact this week as Christ? If we prepare the soil, He can grow the seed (new Christians).

Francis Chan, Crazy Love (Colorado Springs: David C. Cook, 2008), 64-65.

SATISFIED

But whoever has the world's goods, and beholds his brother in need and closes his heart against him, how does the love of God abide in him?

I John 3:17

MY SON JUST UPGRADED HIS little one room home. He changed it from a house with a path to a house with a bath. The older folks will know what I'm talking about. Knowing Dennis is completely happy with what he has keeps my perspectives in order—usually.

When I begin thinking of all the material things people around us have, I start wondering; why can't I have a sun room and a craft room? Or, why can't I have a garage and a storm shelter? The devil likes to hit us where we live.

Lord, help me not to be greedy. Hebrews 13:5 says, "Let your character be free from the love of money, being content with what you have; for He Himself has said, 'I will never desert you, nor will I ever forsake you.'" Thank you, Lord, for granting all my needs and also giving me things beyond my needs! I have made this my daily prayer.

"If a brother or sister is without clothing and in need of daily food, and one of you says to them, 'Go in peace, be warmed and be filled,' and yet you do not give them what is necessary for their body, what use is that? Even so faith, if it has no works, is dead, being by itself" (James 2:15-17).

What if we try to see what we can do this week to make the less fortunate people more comfortable? Do you have two of the same thing but only need one? Give one to the person who is in need.

SAYING YES

A joyful heart is good medicine, but a broken spirit dries up the bones.

Proverbs 17:22

"THAT WAS GOOD, MAMA. CAN we have another piece?" My sons asked with their eyes on the cake.

"No, you'll ruin your supper," I answered to their dismay.

It was the middle of the afternoon. A few minutes before the kids came inside for a break, I had taken a homemade chocolate cake out of the oven. After frosting it, I cut a piece of warm cake for each of us to enjoy. They chattered to me about the fun they were having outside playing with their friends in the dirt, riding their trikes up and down the sidewalk, and looking at bugs—all the things little boys do. But when they asked for some more cake, I said no.

Sometimes we say no because, let's face it, it's just easier! The word yes usually means action will have to be taken on our part. Once in awhile we get so caught up in being a disciplining parent that it gets in the way of the loving parent we should be with our children. The sad fact is that eventually I threw away some of the cake because it had gotten old and lost its flavor.

I look back on this scene time after time. Why didn't I just say, "Sure, a little piece won't hurt"? Then I could have also enjoyed a few more minutes of laughter and closeness with my boys.

In Psalm 103:13, we read, "Just as a father has compassion on his children, so the Lord has compassion on those who fear Him."

What if we answer our child's or grandchild's questions with a yes this week whenever possible and share Jesus with them?

SCRAPBOOKING

But prove yourselves doers of the Word, and not merely hearers who delude themselves.

James 1:22

My SISTER TAUGHT ME THE joy of scrapbooking. It is such a good feeling to be able to give my grandchildren a part of their life history in picture form. I work diligently to make sure everything is placed on the page in correct form before I glue with special scrapbook glue. When the kids come over, they always want to look at their books to see if I've added any new pages. I always take time from my work schedule to devote a few hours for creating and preserving a little history for my grandkids; I enjoy it!

On this vein of thought, there is always some area in the church that needs workers. Ask your church secretary. I'm sure she would have several things for which you could volunteer. Remember, God will not call you to do something without giving you the enthusiasm to do it. God is so good!

We need to remain active in the Lord's work as long as we are able. If we don't do it, who will? James 1:25 declares, "But one who looks intently at the perfect law, the law of liberty, and abides by it, not having become a forgetful hearer but an effectual doer, this man shall be blessed in what he does."

What if I delve into my church responsibilities this week as eagerly as I get into things at home that I love doing? If I volunteer to be a Sunday school teacher or helper, church greeter, or wherever there is a need I can fill, God will give me the desire to do it.

SEEMINGLY USELESS

If we confess our sins, He is faithful and righteous to forgive us our sins and to cleanse us from all unrighteousness.

I John 1:9

THERE WERE TEN GOURDS SITTING on my kitchen table. Betty, my good friend and neighbor, had cleaned them by scraping all the dried weeds and debris from their skin and then told me to take them home and do something with them! As far as I was concerned, they seemed like useless things and shouldn't even have been planted!

I didn't want to let Betty down, so when I arrived home, I went to my computer and typed decorating gourds in the search engine. Instantly, websites appeared wanting my attention. I had no idea there was so much that could be done with gourds! They could be made into geese, bird houses, holiday figures, bowls, and vases. There was a gourd for everything. Some were selling for as much as $75 apiece.

So, with concentrated effort, I tried duplicating some of the easier gourds that were pictured. When the local citizen center's yearly yard sale arrived, I had all the gourds painted as bird houses, happy faces, Santa Claus, and the American Flag. And since it was close to Halloween, I even had some painted as pumpkins with cats on them and goblins with candy in their hands.

Those gourds remind me of myself. God created me and chose me for His own even before I was born. But I was useless to Him until I asked for forgiveness of my sin. "For all have sinned and fall short of the glory of God" (Romans 3:23).

What if I let God know I will be available to Him all week? Then I should be prepared to do willingly what the Lord asks of me!

SPIRITUAL DIET

Do you not know that you are a temple of God, and that the Spirit of God dwells in you? ... For the temple of God is holy, and that is what you are.

I Corinthians 3:16,17b

As soon as I got up this morning, I was in the kitchen with cereal in one hand and milk in the other. I am on a diet, need I say more? Of course, when I can't have bacon and eggs for breakfast, that's what I want! But I know I need to discipline my eating and keep up with the daily exercise. We are always trying to look and feel better physically. It's important we stay healthy physically, but we shouldn't get so caught up in the physical that we neglect the spiritual. It is much more important that our spiritual life is healthy.

The Scripture in this morning's devotional was quite appropriate for me. "Train yourself in godliness, for, while physical training is of some value, godliness is valuable in every way" (I Timothy 4:7-8, NRSV).

I started thinking about my spiritual body. What do I do to keep it in shape? The Scripture just quoted says if we keep our spiritual bodies healthy, we win in every way. Don't forget about godliness training while attempting to maintain healthy physical training.

What if I go to the Scripture and feed my spiritual body several times a day this week just as I do my physical body? Open God's Word whenever there's a spiritual need in your daily life and stay spiritually healthy.

STUMBLING BLOCKS

Commit your works to the Lord and your plans will be established.

Proverbs 16:3

IT WAS TIME ONCE AGAIN to demolish an old car! Bill would bring home an old clunker during county fair month to prepare it for the demolition derby. He and our sons would break out all the glass because it wasn't allowed in the cars participating in the derby. Being five and four years old, they were thrilled at the thought of breaking glass without getting into trouble. The doors were welded shut for safety's sake, and other things were done to compete in the derby.

One day my husband brought home an old Henry J. Bill was going to restore this classic. But when Billy and Jeff saw an old car, they were ecstatic! Another demolition car to fix for Dad! Bill had unknowingly put a stumbling block in their way. In his absence, they went straight to work, knowing what to do—break out all the glass. They even managed to smash one side of the two sectioned windshield. I can say this for them, they were committed to their work!

Their dad went easy on them when he saw the damage to the Ford, knowing the boys thought they had been helping. Bill also realized he should have told them that not all old cars were demolition cars. They were just trying to please their dad and were so proud of themselves!

I compare this incident to the way we conduct ourselves around new Christians. When we are helping them to grow in their faith, let's be sure we don't give them more than they are ready for spiritually. A couple of examples would be expecting them to teach a Sunday school lesson or giving them a list of rules they are to follow other than the Bible. This discourages the new Christian. Compare this to Bill parking the classic auto where the demolition car had been parked earlier; it confused the boys.

Paul has something to say about this problem. "Let us not judge one another, but rather determine this—not to put a stumbling block in a brother's way. ... So then let us pursue the things which make for peace and the building up of one another" (Romans 14:13, 19).

What if I commit my works to the Lord this week and become a stepping stone rather than a stumbling block to others?

SUBSCRIPTIONS

Thus it is not the will of your Father who is in heaven that one of these little ones perish.

Matthew 18:14

A COUPLE OF YEARS AGO, I canceled a subscription to a cooking magazine. I had more than enough recipes to experiment with, so I decided to drop it. You would have thought I had said goodbye to a dear old friend! The company sent me discount coupons for their magazine, urging me to re-subscribe. They said my friends would get a free issue if I gave them another subscription. Each time I received their mail, it would contain a new incentive for me to return.

This made me think about the Bible verse in Luke 15:4-5. "What man among you, if he has a hundred sheep and has lost one of them, does not leave the ninety-nine in the open pasture, and go after the one which is lost, until he finds it? And when he has found it, he lays it on his shoulders, rejoicing."

We need to use every tool God has given us to keep our people in the church as well as remaining active in our outreach programs. We seem to get so caught up in our world of busyness that we miss the little things that Jesus would have us do. How sad it is that people quit coming to church, and we don't even seem to notice they are missing.

What if I called on someone absent from Sunday school or church this week and let them know they were missed? Then I could continue to keep in touch with them with a phone call or take them a treat—or just be a friend! I challenge you to make this one of your new weekly habits.

THE SHIELD
OF FAITH

Do not be afraid of sudden fear, nor of the onslaught of the wicked when it comes; for the Lord will be your confidence, and will keep your foot from being caught.

Proverbs 3:25

HOW MUCH FAITH DO WE really have? This question was asked in our church group one evening. A student said he didn't think we really knew how much faith we have because we've never really had it tested. Have we ever had to depend on God to provide us with food, clothing, or shelter? We live a blessed life.

I was in that category until recently when I experienced some devastating circumstances. Instantly, my income only covered one-third of my monthly expenses. I had no vehicle, and the medical insurance I had for over twenty years was cancelled.

The first week, I panicked! The second week, my common sense kicked in. I knew something had to be done quickly. I poured myself into Bible reading and prayed for some guidance.

God led me to a study book on Proverbs. It gave me confidence and promises galore! My prayers were the most sincere I had ever prayed! God came through!

God was receiving prayers on my behalf from many different people. Answers came from everywhere. Some came immediately, and some came later. God has provided for my needs more than I could ever have imagined.

"In addition to all, taking up the shield of faith with which you will be able to extinguish all the flaming missiles of the evil one" (Ephesians 6:16; emphasis mine). I have heard this verse all my life. I now take it very seriously.

What if every morning this week, we literally act out putting on the armor of God? You will find the full armor in Ephesians 6:11–17.

TOPPLED!

I will lift up my eyes to the mountains; from whence shall
my help come? My help comes from the Lord, who made the
heaven and the earth. He will not allow your foot to slip; He
who keeps you will not slumber.

Psalm 121:1-3

THIS WEEK OUR NEIGHBOR TO the south of us decided to bulldoze his trees down to allow his cattle to have more pasture. Those old oak trees were huge, about sixty feet tall. But when they were up against the bulldozer, it didn't take much to knock them over. When they fell, I discovered the trees' roots were quite shallow compared to the height of the trees. No wonder with one push they were toppled!

This reminded me of some well-known Christians we know and look up to. We try to fashion our Christian lives after their lives. They appear powerful and strong, and it seems nothing can harm them. Then sometimes we find out they have given in to the devil's temptations—whatever they may have been.

James 4:17 says, "Therefore, to one who knows the right thing to do, and does not do it, to him it is sin." If you know there is something that would tempt you to commit sin, then with all the power you have in you, STAY AWAY FROM IT! Our spiritual roots need to go deep into the Word of God.

"To Him who is able to keep you from stumbling, and to make you stand in the presence of His glory blameless with great joy, … be glory, majesty, dominion, and authority before all time and now and forever" (Jude 24-25b).

What if we look to Jesus this week and fashion our lives after Him, the only perfect example?

WAKE UP

You shall love the Lord your God with all your heart, and with all your soul, and with all your strength, and with all your mind; and your neighbor as yourself.

Luke 10:27

HAVE YOU EVER BEEN BEHIND an auto driver who has his blinker signal on but never turns? It's just as bad as being behind one who turns but doesn't use his signal! I wonder what these people are thinking. It's obviously not about their driving. How many times do we catch ourselves just going through life unmindful of the signals we are sending to other people? This is why it is so important to have daily Bible reading and prayer. II Peter 1:5 states, "Now for this very reason also, applying all diligence, in your faith supply moral excellence, and in your moral excellence, knowledge. " This Scripture then continues with the qualities we need so we will not stumble. If you have time, read through verse 15. It will give you encouragement.

Proverbs 12:26 tells us, "The righteous is a guide to his neighbor." But who is our neighbor? I had it explained to me that he is anyone who has a need, whose need I am able to meet. I think that hits the nail on the head, don't you? I'm sure we all know someone who meets this definition. The story of the Good Samaritan is one of my favorite parables. Read Luke 10:30-37 if you want inspiration. This Samaritan lived the Golden Rule.

What if we make sure to give strong godly signals this week to those who may be watching us? We may be the only book these people are reading.

WE ARE THE BRANCHES

Abide in Me, and I in you. As the branch cannot bear fruit of itself, unless it abides in the vine, so neither can you, unless you abide in Me.

John 15:4

IT WAS EARLY MORNING WHEN I strolled out to the garden to see what was ready for picking. My gaze was on the tomatoes and peppers when I noticed the most beautiful flower growing in the midst of the plants. The plant that the flower was growing from was so ugly I just knew it had to be a weed. I picked the produce and went to the house, still thinking about that bloom.

In the afternoon I took my camera to get a close up of this elegant flower, but when I got there, the flower had closed up. I was so disappointed. When my son came over that evening, I asked him if he had noticed the flower since we shared the garden, but he hadn't.

The next day I walked to the garden again just to see if it had re-opened. Do you know what I saw instead of the closed flower? An okra pod was beginning to grow! It was a volunteer okra plant. It was growing in all its glory—a volunteer from the previous year! This incident made me think of the Scripture in John 15:5; "I am the vine, you are the branches; he who abides in Me, and I in him, he bears much fruit; for apart from Me you can do nothing."

What if every morning this week, I prepare, by Bible reading and prayer, to be the most beautiful flower that I can be, on the branch of God's vine? God can make it happen!

WE CANNOT SERVE TWO MASTERS

Now to Him who is able to do exceeding abundantly beyond all that we ask or think, according to the power that works within us, to Him be the glory in the church and in Christ Jesus.

Ephesians 3:20a

IN THE EARLY 1990S, A close friend of mine went through a debilitating divorce. She stayed with me a few months until she could function independently once again.

During her stay, I asked if she would like to know Jesus on a personal level. She explained to me that she was so tired of someone telling her what to do that she wanted to be her own boss for a change. She did not want anyone telling her what to do!

The irony of this statement was that by doing things her way and in her time, she was actually doing what the devil wanted. She was now serving him. The Bible says in Matthew 6:24 that we cannot serve two masters. I have kept in touch with my friend and frequently ask about her salvation. She is not as bitter and angry as she once was, but it still has a hold on her. I pray for her every day, and I send her Christian books to read. I can see she is opening up to the Word of God.

If we repent and give God our heartache and sorrow, He gives us the desires of our heart. And the desire of our heart is to live for Jesus. See how it becomes one and the same?

What if we release our anger and bitterness to God this week and ask Him to forgive us? Then we can truly say we are serving God.

WHEN THE PIECES
DON'T FIT

When you pass through the waters (great trouble), I will be with you; and through the rivers (of difficulty) they will not overflow you. When you walk through the fire you will not be scorched, nor will the flame burn you. For I am the Lord your God.

Isaiah 42:1-3 (words in parentheses are mine)

MY HUSBAND, DALE, IS A stroke survivor. One of the things he did shortly after his return home from his five-week reha-bilitation period at the hospital was to put puzzles together. He would work throughout the day, sometimes only getting five or six pieces together. But he never gave up. Each day he would get a few more connected, and after a few weeks, his puzzle would be completed. I would glue the puzzle pieces together and then pin the puzzle to the wall in his bedroom. Dale really enjoyed looking at his finished puzzles. When he finished a new one, I would replace the old one on the wall. This way, he always had a fresh picture to enjoy.

Dale has since found other things to keep his mind alert. He watches the bird feeder and tells me the types of birds eating from it. He plays Solitaire on the TV game channel, putting the cards in the proper order. But when he was working the puzzles, it reminded me about the times in our lives when the pieces of life's puzzle just don't fit. Nothing seems to work, and we get so discouraged. Think about this. If you look at the bottom side of a puzzle-in-progress, it just looks like a mess of crooked lines. But God sees the top side of the puzzle, our life's work-in-progress, and He knows exactly where the pieces go and the beautiful picture it will produce when He is finished with us.

What if I give any discouraging or difficult matters to God this week? When you pray, try stretching your arms out with palms down releasing all to the Lord. Just the act of doing this will help you realize you have given them to God.

WHEN MISTAKES
NEED FIXED

And do not go on presenting the members of your body to sin as instruments of unrighteousness; but present yourselves to God ... and your members as instruments of righteousness to God. For sin shall not be master over you.

Romans 6:13-14a

KNIT ONE, PURL TWO. DOES this sound familiar? It does if you have ever knitted. This spring I discovered there was a knitting group in my church that met monthly. I knew a lady in the group who knitted her own socks. I wanted to learn to knit, so I asked her if she would teach me.

In the first session, Rose showed me how to put the stitches on the needles and separate them appropriately. This should be easy, I thought. When I got home, I realized it was not.

With no one helping me, I ended up with ten extra stitches on the very next row! I ripped them out and then realized I didn't know how to start over.

When the group met the next month, Rose patiently started me at step one again. This time I paid close attention, and when I made a mistake, she showed me how to correct the error. However, when it was just a small problem, she would fix it for me so I could continue knitting.

Sometimes when I make mistakes in my Christian life, God says, "That's okay, I can fix it," and I go on following Him. But sometimes, when I really mess up, I need to go to the Lord and ask Him to forgive me for disobeying and make restitution, if needed.

What if I go to my Savior this week as soon as I realize I have done wrong and pray for Him to help me? This will keep my relationship with Him alive and well!

For more information about
Ruth Perry
&
What If
please visit:

ruthperrya.wordpress.com
ruthperry@centurytel.net
facebook.com/inspired.ones

For more information about
AMBASSADOR INTERNATIONAL
please visit:

www.ambassador-international.com
@AmbassadorIntl
www.facebook.com/AmbassadorIntl